The
Norman Rockwell
Museum
at Stockbridge

The Norman Rockwell Museum at Stockbridge
Stockbridge, Massachusetts 01262

Triple Self-Portrait (cover), Oil on canvas, *Saturday Evening Post* cover 1960
Deadline (top), Oil on canvas, *Saturday Evening Post* cover 1938

The Norman Rockwell Museum at Stockbridge

I am pleased to have this opportunity to acquaint you with the Norman Rockwell Museum at Stockbridge. This guidebook will take you on a pictorial journey over the museum's grounds, and show you some of the highlights of the collections.

The museum exhibits the largest public collections of artwork by Norman Rockwell. Inspired by the legacy of Norman Rockwell, the museum is dedicated to the advancement of art appreciation and education. The museum preserves, studies and communicates to a worldwide audience the life, art and spirit of Rockwell's work in the field of illustration. The museum is also committed to interpreting the broad themes of Rockwell's contributions to illustration, American popular culture and society. Visitors find this a friendly gathering place to discover, enjoy and study the artist's work.

Norman Rockwell helped found the museum, and his family and estate continue to endorse it. The museum is a not-for-profit educational institution that evolved by popular demand and continues to grow in response to the needs of its local, national and international audiences. In 1967, a group of Stockbridge citizens that included Norman Rockwell and his wife, Molly, formed an organization that purchased the Old Corner House, an historic home on

Based on the theme of a New England town hall, architect Robert A.M. Stern's wood, slate and fieldstone building (top) reflects local architectural traditions.

Peter Rockwell's bronze bust of his father (bottom) inscribed *N.R. by P.R.*, is displayed in the terrace gallery of the museum.

Main Street, Stockbridge, that was threatened with demolition.

In 1969, the Old Corner House opened to the public with exhibits from the town library's historical collection and Norman Rockwell offered to lend several paintings to the exhibition. Gradually, through word of mouth, the Old Corner House became identified as a center for the exhibition of original Rockwell works, and about 5,000 people had visited by the end of its first year.

In 1973, Rockwell left his art in trust to the museum to ensure the collection's future public exhibition and care. This collection, known as the Norman Rockwell Art Collection Trust, became the foundation of the Norman Rockwell Museum collections. Three years later, he added his studio and its contents to the trust. In that same year of 1976, the museum began a ten-year research project that resulted in the 1986 publication of *Norman Rockwell: A Definitive Catalogue*, which catalogues more than 3,500 images by Rockwell. Today the museum houses the artist's papers and archives, and is recognized as a center of research and scholarship on Rockwell.

In 1993, the museum moved into a new state-of-the-art building designed by architect Robert A.M. Stern, located on a former estate in Stockbridge. The museum complex at the 36-acre Linwood site welcomes more than 250,000 visitors annually. In keeping with his wish that his working

A photographic mural of *Stockbridge Main Street at Christmas* (top) welcomes visitors to the museum's lobby.

Spacious galleries (bottom) are home to both permanent and changing exhibitions.

environment be shared with the public, Norman Rockwell's studio with its contents was moved in 1986 from Rockwell's home in the center of Stockbridge to the new site, and is now open to museum visitors from May through October. Rolling lawns and beautiful vistas invite you to stroll and picnic on the grounds among the sculptures by Peter Rockwell that dot the landscape.

The museum exhibits year-round many of its master works by Rockwell such as *Stockbridge Main Street at Christmas*, *Four Freedoms* and *Triple Self-Portrait*. Rotating exhibits from the permanent collections, and exhibitions of the works of other illustrators complete the museum's active exhibition schedule. Public programs featuring lectures and art classes by noted contemporary illustrators and artists make the museum a vibrant center for the study of visual communication. The beauty of the Berkshire's four distinct seasons and its abundance of cultural attractions turn a visit to the Norman Rockwell Museum into a lifetime experience.

I hope that this guidebook will be a reminder of what you have enjoyed on your visit here, or will be an enticing overview of what awaits you when you come to the Norman Rockwell Museum.

Laurie Norton Moffatt, Director
The Norman Rockwell Museum
at Stockbridge

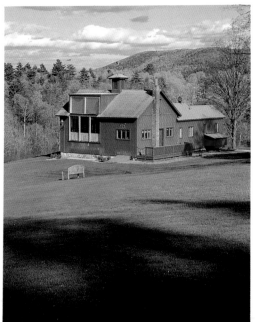

The studio (top) with its original contents in place, as it was left by Norman Rockwell.

In 1976, Rockwell placed his studio (left) and its contents in trust to the museum. Moved from the artist's home in Stockbridge center to the museum site in 1986, it is open to the public from May through October.

Norman Rockwell's studio (top) in the
Berkshire hills of Massachusetts.

Rockwell in his studio (left), with the completed painting *Peace Corps (JFK's Bold
Legacy)* painted in 1966 for *Look* magazine.

"I showed the America I knew and observed to others who might not have noticed."

Norman Rockwell

Norman Rockwell with *Freedom to Worship,* c. 1967.

Norman Rockwell is the artist Americans know best. Millions of people saw each of his cover illustrations for the *Saturday Evening Post.* He worked for every major magazine over a period of almost 70 years and was commissioned to paint the portrait of every major presidential candidate from 1952 to 1972. Rockwell's subject matter ranged from product advertising to sensitive social issues. His work has been reproduced to a phenomenal degree, and his name has become a synonym for the small-town values he so often depicted. Although his last commissioned work was published in 1976, his reputation continues to grow.

Perhaps the most obvious reason for the popularity of Rockwell's work is its subject matter—he painted America and Americans. His themes are rooted in American values and our pride in those values. He did not seek out the ugly or the sordid but chose to accentuate the positive in the American character. Rockwell himself said, "I paint life as I would like it to be."

The American family was at the core of Norman Rockwell's work. His view of family life remains compelling to us today because he painted universal situations and relationships—those aspects of family life that transcend history. Rockwell's empathy with his subjects and his attention to detail combined to produce a picture of ourselves that is at once authentic and nostalgic.

Norman Rockwell covered the significant events of twentieth-century America and the people who helped shape our world. During World War II, he created the images that became symbols for a nation at war: Willie Gillis and Rosie the Riveter. He portrayed the civil rights struggle and other moral issues in ways all Americans could understand. His portraits of public personalities range from Charles Lindbergh to Neil Armstrong, Harry Truman to Ronald Reagan, early Gary Cooper to late John Wayne.

Norman Percevel Rockwell was born in New York City on February 3, 1894, the second child of Nancy and Jarvis Waring Rockwell. Norman and his brother Jarvis enjoyed the urban pastimes of playing stickball and chasing fire engines, but also delighted in the summers that the family spent on a farm in upstate New York. In his writing and illustrations as an adult, Rockwell idealized country life and compared it to what he saw as the sordid atmosphere of the city. The Rockwells remained in New York City until 1903, when the family moved to Mamaroneck, New York.

As a boy, Norman Rockwell was nonathletic, clumsy, skinny, and pigeon-toed.

An early photograph of Rockwell with two young models outside his New Rochelle studio, 1925.

However, he could draw, and his ambition, even as a youngster, was to be an illustrator. In 1909, Rockwell left high school to study art full-time, briefly attending the National Academy of Design before enrolling at the Art Students League in New York City.

Rockwell found success early. He painted his first commission—four Christmas cards—before his sixteenth birthday. At the age of 18, Rockwell began doing illustrations for *Boys' Life,* a new magazine published by the Boy Scouts of America. Within a few months, he became art director for the magazine. Although he served as art director for only a few years, his association with the Boy Scouts was lifelong. He illustrated the first Boy Scout *Hike* and *Camp* books as well as many story illustrations that appeared in *Boys' Life* magazine. In addition, he began a successful freelance career working for a variety of publications.

By 1915, Rockwell had moved to New Rochelle, New York, where he established his own studio with the celebrated cartoonist Clyde Forsythe. At the time, New Rochelle was home to a number of well-known illustrators including J.C. and Frank Leyendecker, Coles Phillips and Howard Chandler Christy. Rockwell's illustrations soon began appearing in well-known maga-

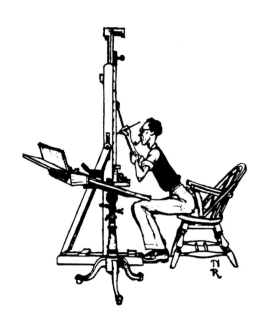

For the 1946 *Post* cover, *Crestwood Commuter Station*, Norman Rockwell poses as a commuter racing to catch a train.

zines such as *Country Gentleman*, *Literary Digest*, and the children's magazine *St. Nicholas*. His first *Saturday Evening Post* cover, *Boy with Baby Carriage,* appeared on May 20, 1916. This was the first of 321 covers he would create for the *Post*, the most popular magazine of its day, and marked the beginning of an association which would last for 47 years.

Rockwell married Irene O'Connor in 1916, a marriage that would end in divorce in 1929. Two years after his marriage, he enlisted in the navy, serving at the Charleston, South Carolina Naval Reserve Base during World War I. Rockwell had no official military duties; he was the art editor for *Afloat and Ashore*, the base publication, and painted portraits of naval officers. Since he was permitted to do his own work, Rockwell illustrations continued to appear in the *Post* and other magazines during the war. His scenes of soldiers on shipboard and singing around the campfire reminded the folks at home of the boys "Over There."

The 1920s found Rockwell back in New Rochelle. Although he continued to work for the leading publications of the day, illustrating new products, from automobiles to raisins, now made up a substantial part of his work. In 1925, the first in a series of Boy Scout calendars with Rockwell illustrations

appeared; the series would run for more than 50 years. While many of his magazine covers during the 1920s continued to focus on children caught in comic escapades, others chronicled the changing times: women voting for president for the first time, Lindbergh after his historic flight, the advent of radio, and the increasing number of automobiles on the road.

In 1930, Rockwell met and married Mary Barstow, a young school teacher from California. The couple had three sons: Jarvis, Thomas, and Peter. The decade of the 1930s was one of the richest of Rockwell's career. While he continued to do covers for the *Post* and calendars for the Boy Scouts, many of his most beloved story and book illustrations were completed during this period. In 1935, he received a commission from the Heritage Press to illustrate Mark Twain's classics, *The Adventures of Tom Sawyer* and *The Adventures of Huckleberry Finn*, creating images that, for many people, portrayed these two characters definitively.

Looking for a change of scene and a better environment in which to raise their three young sons, the Rockwell family moved to Arlington, Vermont, in 1939, and Rockwell's work began to reflect small town American life more consistently. He remarked that "I guess I have a bad case of the

American nostalgia for the clean, simple country life as opposed to the complicated world of the city."

During World War II, Rockwell's illustrations of "armchair generals" and women war-workers depicted life on the home front. Willie Gillis, Rockwell's fictional G.I., made his first appearance in 1941 and was featured in 11 *Post* covers, including a 1946 cover showing Willie at college, presumably on the G.I. Bill. Soldiers were shown at home on leave, on KP duty, and riding troop trains. Only one Rockwell image, a factory production poster, showed a soldier on the front lines, sitting at a machine gun that is almost out of ammunition.

The *Four Freedoms*, Rockwell's most famous paintings of the period and among his most significant works, were completed in 1943 and served as his contribution to the war effort. The paintings were based on Franklin D. Roosevelt's 1941 speech, and illustrate the basic freedoms—freedom of speech, freedom to worship, freedom from want, and freedom from fear—for which Americans were fighting. Published in the *Post* with essays on each freedom by respected writers and philosophers, the paintings created an immediate sensation. They became symbols of the nation and the centerpiece of the government's second war

bond drive that toured the country in an exhibition sponsored by the *Post* and the U.S. Treasury Department to sell war bonds. This traveling exhibition was seen by more than 1.2 million people and raised more than $130 million for the war effort.

The year 1943 also represented a great loss for Rockwell when his Arlington studio burned to the ground. Rockwell lost three decades worth of research and reference material, a collection of hundreds of costumes and props, an unknown number of original paintings and drawings, and even his favorite pipes. Admirers from around the country sent him replacement pipes, the Society of Illustrators replaced his collection of prints, and the Treasury Department even sent him a copy of the citation it had awarded him for the *Four Freedoms*. Although the loss was devastating, Rockwell eventually decided that it had forcibly given him a new start in his work, causing him to take a fresh look at things rather than turning to his picture files. Illustrator Mead Schaeffer, Rockwell's close friend, joked, "He was so damned convincing that for several weeks I was on the point of burning down my own studio."

During the post-war years, Rockwell continued to chronicle American life on the cover of the *Saturday Evening Post*. The cov-

Two American icons, Norman Rockwell and John Wayne, pose during a working session for a portrait commissioned by the National Cowboy Hall of Fame, 1974.

ers done during this period, including *Christmas Homecoming*, *Girl at the Mirror*, *Marriage License*, and *The Runaway*, are among Rockwell's most well-known and beloved illustrations. In addition, he produced a large number of advertising and commercial illustrations, such as a series of Christmas cards for Hallmark, and advertisements for Ford Motor Company and the Massachusetts Mutual Life Insurance Company. In 1948, Rockwell did his first illustrations for the *Four Seasons* Brown and Bigelow calendar, a series that would continue for seventeen years.

In 1953, Rockwell and his family moved to Stockbridge, Massachusetts, where Mary Barstow Rockwell died six years later. *My Adventures as An Illustrator*, an autobiography he wrote in collaboration with his son, Tom, was published in 1960. The *Saturday Evening Post* excerpted portions of the book in a series of articles, one of which featured the famous *Triple Self-Portrait* on the cover. In 1961, Rockwell met Mary (Molly) Punderson, a retired schoolteacher who was leading a poetry class that Rockwell had joined. They were married later that year.

Norman Rockwell's last *Post* cover was published in 1963. A new association with *Look* magazine produced illustrations depicting the major events and social trends of the day. Rockwell's first *Look* illustration, *The Problem We All Live With*, published in 1964, spotlights school desegregation. Other topics included the space race and the war in the Middle East. "There was a change of the thought climate in America brought on by the scientific advances, the atom bomb, two world wars, and Mr. Freud and psychology," Rockwell wrote in a draft of a lecture around 1966. "Now I am wildly excited about painting contemporary subject [sic] ... pictures about civil rights, astronauts, Peace Corps, poverty program. It's wonderful!"

Rockwell continued to paint through the mid-1970s, although he cut back on the number of commissions he accepted. At the age of 82, as the United States celebrated its bicentennial, Rockwell completed his last cover illustration and saw the publication of his final Boy Scout calendar. With great affection for their neighbor, the people of Stockbridge honored Rockwell with a parade in celebration of the Bicentennial. In early 1977, he was awarded perhaps his highest honor, the Presidential Medal of Freedom, by President Gerald R. Ford for his "vivid and affectionate portraits of our country." He died at his home in Stockbridge on November 8, 1978.

We remember Norman Rockwell as a recorder of contemporary American life. During the early twentieth century, illustrations played as large a role in shaping America's self-image as they did in portraying it. More than 4,000 works of art by Rockwell are known. These images became a defining influence on several generations of Americans, and the term "Norman Rockwell" has come to connote a certain type of small-town atmosphere and spirit of gentle humor and fair play. Norman Rockwell's legacy as the premier illustrator of the 20th century brought the art of illustration into virtually every home in America.

Family Tree, Oil on canvas, *Saturday Evening Post* cover 1959. Although this family tree is fictional, it is a telling look at America's heritage. Rockwell traced family resemblances and traits through a series of generations. The variety of cultural and historic influences gives this painting its appeal.

Boy With Baby Carriage, Oil on canvas, *Saturday Evening Post* cover 1916. This was the first of 321 *Saturday Evening Post* covers Rockwell painted in his 47-year association with the magazine. The fact that one model posed for all three boys shows Rockwell's ability to create distinctive characters.

No Swimming, Oil on canvas, *Saturday Evening Post* cover 1921. Rockwell's depictions of childhood are universally understood and appreciated. With his story-telling ability and technical mastery, viewers can sense both the urgency of flight and the soft texture of the puppy's fur.

Outward Bound, Oil on canvas. *Ladies' Home Journal* 1927. This touching illustration is created through the juxtaposition of onlookers and adventurers, youth and old age, land and sea. Rockwell's play of light and dark emphasizes these contrasts.

Aunt Ella Takes a Trip (top), Oil on canvas, *Ladies' Home Journal* story illustration 1942. "...in illustration, one strives more for atmosphere, and can approach the esthetic standards of the fine artist..."—Norman Rockwell. In this story illustration about a young girl's visit to her aunt and uncle, Rockwell uses light in an impressionistic way to create the atmosphere of a bright summer day in the country.

Spring Flowers (bottom), Oil on canvas, *McCall's* 1969. Rockwell's only still-life, *Spring Flowers*, was inspired by his third wife, Molly. By using her sun hat, gardening gloves and sneakers, Rockwell portrays Molly's presence without painting her directly.

Youth and Old Age, Oil on canvas, Colgate Dental Cream advertisement 1924. Rockwell's advertisement for Colgate Dental Cream employs a narrative scene. Focusing on the wisdom imparted from one generation to another, the caption read, "If your wisdom teeth could talk, they'd say 'Use Colgate's.'"

The Book of Romance (top)**,** Oil on canvas, *Ladies' Home Journal* 1927. This painting is an example of Rockwell's "subject" pictures where a quieter image lacks the more immediate impact of a cover illustration. The works themselves were the story since they appeared in magazines without accompanying text. The elderly gentleman in the foreground experiences romance through books while a young romance is unfolding in the back room.

Gossips, Oil on canvas, *Saturday Evening Post* cover 1948. While the idea for this *Post* cover came to Rockwell in the 1920s, the task of painting so many portraits made the artist shy away from it for nearly twenty years. The humorous twist to this story of gossip is its victim, Rockwell himself.

Checkers, Oil on canvas, *Ladies' Home Journal* story illustration 1928. The circus theme provided Rockwell with an endless variety of characters to portray. The drama, make-up, costumes and lifestyle were well suited to the artist's brand of visual storytelling. In this story, circus performers conspire to renew the confidence of the disheartened clown through a high-stakes game of checkers.

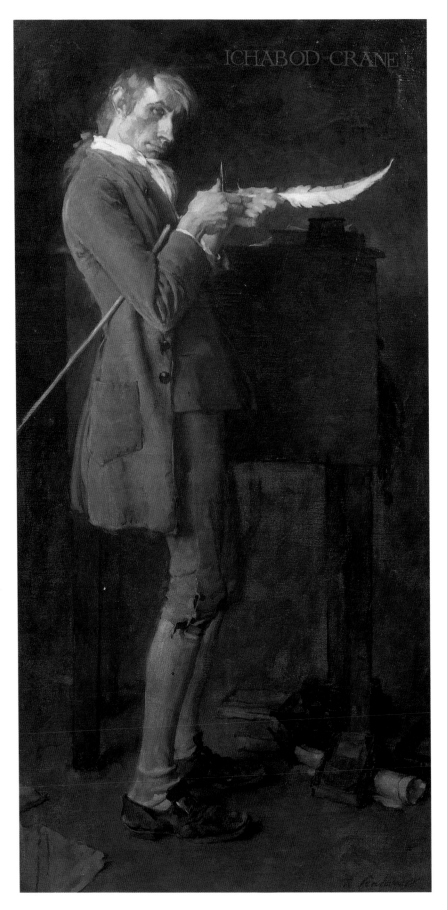

Ichabod Crane, Oil on canvas, c. 1937. *Ichabod Crane* was created as one in a series of illustrations of celebrated characters in American fiction. The painting is an example of Rockwell's attention to historical accuracy as depicted by the costumes and props.

Thanksgiving—Ye Glutton, Oil on canvas, *Life* cover 1923. Norman Rockwell was commissioned to illustrate covers for a variety of magazines including this image for *Life*, then a humor magazine. For the Thanksgiving issue, the artist portrayed a pilgrim paying for his gluttonous behavior.

Going and Coming, Oil on canvas, *Saturday Evening Post* cover 1947. This unique *Post* cover created on two canvases tells the story of a family outing. The contrasting moods from eagerness and anticipation to exhaustion and fulfillment invite comparison, although one character remains resigned throughout.

Family Grace, Oil on canvas. *Ladies' Home Journal* story illustration 1938. In his story illustrations, Norman Rockwell chose to portray the moments in the narrative that most appealed to him or those that captured the essence of a situation. In this image, a city boy visits his grandparents in the country and recalls " his mother's caution about waiting for the prayer."

THE FOUR FREEDOMS

Freedom of Speech, Oil on canvas, *Saturday Evening Post* 1943. "I'll illustrate the *Four Freedoms* using my Vermont neighbors as models. I'll express the ideas in simple everyday scenes. *Freedom of Speech*—a New England town meeting. *Freedom from Want*—a Thanksgiving Dinner. Take them out of the noble language of the proclamation and put them in terms everybody can understand." —Norman Rockwell

Freedom to Worship, Oil on canvas, *Saturday Evening Post* 1943. "I am grateful for the reproductions of Norman Rockwell's paintings illustrating the *Four Freedoms*. He has done a superb job in bringing home the plain, everyday truths behind them." —President Franklin D. Roosevelt

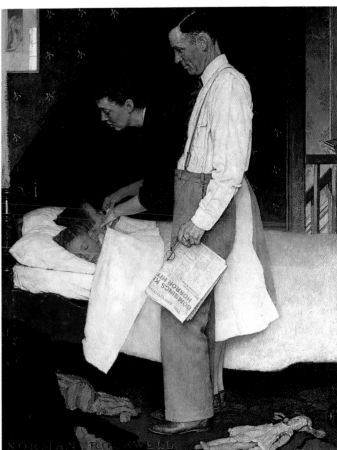

Freedom from Want, Oil on canvas, *Saturday Evening Post* 1943. "These four pictures quickly became the best known and most appreciated paintings of that era. The . . . American people needed the inspirational message which they conveyed so forcefully and so beautifully." —Ben Hibbs, editor, *Saturday Evening Post*

Freedom from Fear, Oil on canvas, *Saturday Evening Post* 1943. "It remained for you to capture the real spirit of 'The Four Freedoms' as it lives in the hearts of the plain people of America. Yours is easily the most moving appeal of all the appeals directed at the winning of the war, and I am proud to know the man whose brush is responsible for it." —Letter to Norman Rockwell

Christmas Homecoming, Oil on canvas, *Saturday Evening Post* cover 1948. The whole Rockwell family appears in this 1948 *Post* cover. Wife Mary embraces son Jarvis, while Norman, middle son Tom (plaid shirt) and youngest son Peter (far left in glasses) look on. Grandma Moses and illustrator Mead Schaeffer also appear.

Norman Rockwell with friend and fellow artist, Grandma Moses, at her 89th birthday party, 1949.

Mary Whalen, a neighbor in Arlington, Vermont, was one of Rockwell's favorite models because she could assume any expression he requested, 1952.

Girl at the Mirror, Oil on canvas, *Saturday Evening Post* cover 1954. This Rockwell *Post* cover depicts the universal theme of coming of age. "I should not have added the photograph of the movie star. The little girl is not wondering if she looks like the star, but just trying to estimate her own charms." —Norman Rockwell

Marriage License, Oil on canvas, *Saturday Evening Post* cover 1955. Visual clues such as facial expressions, body language and props are the keys to interpreting Rockwell paintings including the *Marriage License*. The clerk is eager to go home, while a young couple linger over their marriage license. Notice how the details support the story.

A shopkeeper and a local engaged couple (bottom) pose in Stockbridge Town Hall, 1955.

Saying Grace, Oil on canvas, *Saturday Evening Post* cover 1951. *Saying Grace* was voted by millions of *Post* readers as their favorite cover. Once called a quiet sermon in paint, it is one of the few paintings inspired by a fan's suggestion.

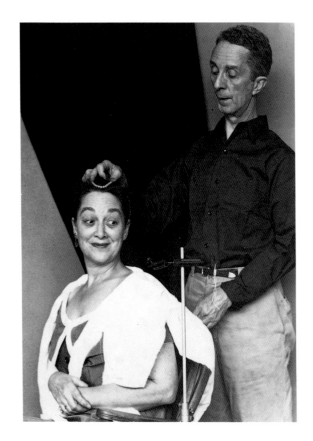

Pencil on paper

Oil on acetate on board

Norman Rockwell poses wife Mary (top left) as the elegant lady in the *Art Critic*, 1955.

Art Critic, *Saturday Evening Post* cover 1955. Rockwell's creative process is well documented in this series of pencil and oil sketches leading to a completed *Post* cover. The idea sketch would be followed by modeling sessions and gathering reference material. Studies of composition and color followed. In the final painting, the viewer can see how the idea has evolved.

Oil on canvas

The Runaway, Oil on canvas, *Saturday Evening Post* cover 1958. *The Runaway* was inspired by Rockwell's own experience as a boy in Mamaroneck, New York. Rockwell commented that by setting it at a rural lunch counter, he portrayed the idea that the boy " had got well out of town before being apprehended." The amused counterman is shown as an understanding and experienced type.

After the Prom, Oil on canvas, *Saturday Evening Post* cover 1957. Rockwell said he had an irresistible impulse to caricature the faces in this painting. A familiar setting and common experience combined with the theme of young love made this one of the artist's most nostalgic *Post* covers.

Stockbridge Main Street at Christmas, Oil on canvas, *McCall's* 1967. This loving portrait of Rockwell's last hometown was begun in the mid-1950s and completed for *McCall's* magazine in 1967. To modernize the image, dated by its 50s-style automobiles, he added two 60s-style cars, one entering and one leaving town. Taking artistic liberty, Rockwell included his own home off Main Street and added the Berkshire Hills to the background. "I just love Stockbridge. I mean, Stockbridge is the best of America, the best of New England."

Norman Rockwell in his studio with *Stockbridge Main Street at Christmas*, 1967.

DO UNTO OTHERS
AS YOU WOULD HAVE THEM
DO UNTO YOU

Golden Rule, Oil on canvas, *Saturday Evening Post* cover 1961. Rockwell believed in the golden rule, and his artwork in the 1960s reflected his dedication to global peace and harmony. "I wanted to include people of every race, creed, and color, depicting them with dignity and respect."

Peace Corps (JFK's Bold Legacy), Oil on canvas, *Look* 1966. In the 1960s, Norman Rockwell became increasingly interested in painting international issues. This illustration for *Look* magazine introduced Rockwell's pictorial essay on the Peace Corps. By positioning John F. Kennedy as leading the volunteers, the artist indicates that the Peace Corps will always belong to the late president.

The Problem We All Live With (top), Oil on canvas, *Look* 1964. This depiction of school desegregation was an illustration for *Look* magazine. Rockwell directs attention to the little girl by placing her in the center of the action and omitting the faces of the U.S. Marshalls who escort her to school.

Norman Rockwell with *Lincoln, the Railsplitter* (bottom) a 1964 advertisement for Lincoln Savings Bank.

Lincoln for the Defense, Oil on canvas, *Saturday Evening Post* story illustration 1962. Abraham Lincoln was Norman Rockwell's favorite American and was pictured in many of his paintings. By placing the viewer's perspective at the feet of Lincoln, Rockwell emphasizes the stature and dignity of the man in this depiction of a historic legal defense.

Linwood House was built in 1859 for New York attorney Charles Butler. The "cottage" now serves as the administrative offices for the museum.

Norman Rockwell's youngest son, Peter, created playful sculptures that dot the museum landscape. The element of humor found in his work is as important to him as it was to his father.

Acknowledgements
All images and drawings reproduced with the kind permission of the Norman Rockwell Family Trust.

Book Credits
This book copyright © 1995 by The Norman Rockwell Museum at Stockbridge, may not be reproduced in any form, in whole or part, without the written permission of The Norman Rockwell Museum at Stockbridge.

Concept and design copyright © 1995 by Fort Church Publishers, Inc., Little Compton, R.I. 02837

Curatorial services by Maureen Hart Hennessey

Archival research by Linda Szekely

Production by Marnie Boardman

Edited by James B. Patrick

Designed by Donald G. Paulhus

Published by Fort Church Publishers, Inc., Little Compton, R.I. 02837

Printed in China

Distributed by The Norman Rockwell Museum at Stockbridge, Stockbridge, Massachusetts 01262.
Telephone 413-298-4100.